HOW TO HELP

NATURE SPIRITS

CLEAN UP THE

ENVIRONMENT

by

Clifford J. Mikkelson

Golden Gnome Press

For additional information write to:
      Golden Gnome Press
      P.O. Box 189
      Birch Tree, MO   65438

Illustrations by Doris Hire and Cliff Mikkelson

Published by the Golden Gnome Press

Library of Congress Catalog Card Number: 96-75511
ISBN: 0-9651249-0-8

Printed in the United States of America

Printed in the USA by

*M*₂₀RRIS
PUBLISHING
3212 E. Hwy 30
Kearney, NE 68847
800-650-7888

ACKNOWLEDGMENTS

I am expressing my gratitude to Rose Ford for helping me with the typing of the manuscript; to Harvey M. Haeberle for some editing and layout suggestions and for getting the manuscript ready for printing; to my son Christopher for helping me to get in touch with the innocence of early childhood; and to my troop of twelve nature spirits who inspire me to do something every day for and with elemental life and the environment.

About the Author

Cliff Mikkelson has been consciously cooperating with nature spirits for more than 20 years. He has spent a lot of time outdoors in the Ozarks of Arkansas and Missouri, the seashores of California, the mountains of California, Wyoming, and Montana, and the jungles of Borneo. He lives on a beautiful ranch in the Missouri Ozarks with his son Christopher and other friends who love the outdoors and the nature spirits.

DEDICATION

I respectfully dedicate this book to all elemental life—
the gnomes, sylphs, undines and salamanders who
have worked so joyfully and diligently to make our
planet earth a beautiful home.

THE SWEET PEA FAIRY

In the morning, just as the sun comes up,
The Sweet Pea fairy flitters up and down the vine,
Awakening all the sweet pea flowers with a cheery cup
Of sunlight essence processed through dew drops that shine
And glisten with the first rays of morning light.
The delicate flowers dressed in blue, pink, and white,
Rub their sleepy eyes and straighten their stems,
Appearing just like beauty queens who have a natural grace.
The Sweet Pea fairy is proud of her little gems
Who adorn the elegant vine, each one with a smiling face.
They are ready for another day to brighten the border
And to glorify their creator who designed their patterns.
The Sweet Pea fairy has only to keep them in order
And to keep harmonizing the   cycles in their turns,
For some will fade away, and some will make seeds
As others bloom forth to replace the one's who have gone.
Onward they grow, onward they go, as each one heeds
The fairy's loving touch, as gentle as the dewy dawn.
Peace, beauty, and harmony fill her long-lived days
As she fashions flowers with energy from the sun's rays.

INTRODUCTION

THE ECOLOGY MOVEMENT

The ecology movement is going on strongly now. Children learn about ecology in school. They learn about recycling and the importance of preserving our environment. Industrial captains are paying attention to their effects on the environment. Many companies boast of their role in recycling products and conservation efforts. Politicians vie with each other in having the most regard for the environment. Almost everyone seems to be aware that we need to take care of our environment.

PLEASE INCLUDE THE NATURE SPIRITS

We are making progress in lots of ways in taking care of our earth, and we still have a long way to go, but we are ignoring some of our best helpers in cleaning up and beautifying the earth—namely the nature spirits of earth, air, fire, and water.

I've been to many Earth Day celebrations and have read about many more, but seldom have I heard any talk about the nature spirits and their role in cleaning up the environment.

Public opinion surveys have shown that many people believe in the existence of angels. Although they may not have seen any, many people have felt the presence of angels. Many people also believe in the reality of nature spirits—the gnomes, elves, fairies, sylphs, mermaids and so on, but the folklore coming down from European traditions has clouded over the actual roles that the nature spirits play in our earth drama; so most people don't seem to take them seriously, and don't believe they have anything to do with our lives, especially in our high tech western world. However, thanks to such places as Findhorn, Perelandra, and the Royal Teton Ranch, some people have been communicating with angels and nature spirits and they have helped rekindle a serious interest in the work of nature spirits.

This little booklet starts with the premise that nature spirits do exist, and that they work under the direction of God and the hierarchy of angels and Elohim. (The Elohim being the seven creative spirits of God who help build the myriad forms of the universe.)

EXPERIMENT WITH TRUTH

If you don't believe in them, I urge you to experiment with an open mind. Ideas for experiments will be given in the second chapter. If you're a half-way believer, I urge you to believe one hundred percent and discover how many results you will see. And if you already believe or know for certain that nature spirits exist, I urge you to work with them in healing the earth. The earth is also their home, and they care about it as much as we do—maybe even more than we do, because they are more in touch with the animating spirit in everything.

THE NATURE SPIRITS WANT OUR HELP

The nature spirits are partially dependent on our thoughts and actions. God created them as our servants in a way. They are eager to help us and they have been helping us all along the way. They know that the earth needs to be cleaned up, but they want us to recognize and appreciate their efforts and to take them into partnership with them.

This booklet will give you an introduction to nature spirits—the different types, the work they do, and how you can work with them to improve the world we live in—the planet we live on.

CHAPTER ONE

**"This is truth: As from a fire aflame
thousands of sparks come forth,
even so from the Creator an infinity
of beings have life and to him return again."**
-Mundaka Upanishad

THE ELEMENTAL NATURE SPIRITS

God has created the different kinds of nature spirits to go along with the four basic elements that constitute nature—fire, air, water, and earth. That's why nature spirits are also called elementals. The elementals of earth are called gnomes. The water elementals are called undines. Elementals of air are called sylphs. And salamanders are the elementals of fire. By the way, the little amphibious creatures called salamanders were so named because it was thought that they could live in fire—just like the salamanders do.

Within each category there are different types and variations of nature spirits. For example, elves, brownies, leprechauns, flower fairies, and mannikins work with the earth element; so they would be in the category of gnomes. There are also specific kinds of nature spirits that are called gnomes who work with rocks, gems and underground processes of nature.

Sea sprites, mermaids, and water babies are in the category of undines. Within the category of sylphs are the cloud spirits, storm spirits, and the sylphs who are very close to being angels. The fiery salamanders range from little candle salamanders to the forty or fifty foot tall rainbow colored salamanders seen in forest fires and volcanoes.

THE FORMS OF NATURE SPIRITS

The nature spirits are in between spirit and matter. They are not ghosts or spirits without bodies connected to earth. They do have material bodies, but they are invisible to our normal vision. They have personalities and their bodies resemble humans, but sometimes and some kinds of nature spirits resemble animals. Their bodies are not solid—they are more like holograms—pictures of light, but having some actual substance finer than rarest gases.

Solid objects of earth do not block them. They can go right through stone or into the earth or water as easily as we can walk through a shadow. They can change the appearance of their bodies to suit their fancy or according to what work they happen to be doing. Gnomes often take human beings as their fashion models. Gnomes seen in Europe often look like European peasants, but gnomes seen in America may resemble Indians. They don't seem to change fashions very quickly, because they do use our own thought forms that are projected toward them—and the nature spirits have been pretty much ignored in the 20th century.

As far as size goes, the nature spirits range from the tiny half-inch grass elementals to the huge dragon-like air elementals that span the upper reaches of the atmosphere. Most of the gnomes, undines, and salamanders are six inches to two or three feet tall.

Most of the sylphs are about the size of adult human beings. There are wide variations in every category. For another example, huge undines with gorilla-like bodies dwell out in the depths of the ocean.

The bodies of the nature spirits work with a chakra system. Just as we have our system of seven chakras to receive and distribute spiritual energy, so the nature spirits have one or more chakras that sustain their existence.

Nature spirits are "born" into the world by the creative power of Elohim and angels. They may live for hundreds or thousands of years, then they pass on.

THE FUNCTIONS OF NATURE SPIRITS

The nature spirits are agents of God to keep the material creation functioning properly. They act as transformers and transmitters of God's creative energy. God is sending energy to this planet through the sun and through the great central suns of the galaxy and the universe. The nature spirits absorb the sunlight and the cosmic energy and magnetic rays from God, assimilate it, and then discharge it to the earth and all living things, mineral, vegetable, and animal life. It's a cycle they continuously go through. It brings them great joy—even ecstasy to do this. Just as God is blissful, the nature spirits share in the bliss as they absorb, assimilate and discharge cosmic energy.

This is important to remember when you are consciously working with the nature spirits—they are full of joy and like to play as they work and work as they play—indeed, there's no difference. It's all the same to them, as it is with us when we enjoy what we're doing.

However, and here we come to the crux of the problem, the nature spirits do have to deal with the negative energies created by human beings—cruel acts, hate, envy, cursings, unkind words, etc. coalesce into negative force fields that affect life on this planet. The nature spirits have to bear the burden to keep the earth in harmony for us. When there is too much negativity as in wars, riots and mass campaigns of hatred, then there may be too much negativity for the nature spirits and the angels to handle, in which case the collective whole of the nature spirits—Mother Nature—may have to adjust things with storms, earthquakes, floods, or other "natural" disasters. And the worse conditions are, the greater the potential for catastrophe. Such was the fate of ancient Atlantis. When things got so bad, so out of divine order, the only way left to handle the situation was to sink the whole continent, the island continent of Atlantis. It's now below the ocean water.

There have been many prophecies of the earth being in danger of going through major cataclysms within the next 25 years or even 10 years; so it is very important that we learn to work with the nature spirits in restoring harmony, peace, justice, and love on this earth. The prophetic voices have also said that disasters need not happen. We can change our environment for the better.

THE NATURE SPIRITS PLACE IN HIERARCHY

God is the ultimate in being organized of course, so the nature spirits have their place in life, and work under the direction of angels and angel devas, who have their own organized set-up. The angel devas are the ones who supervise and work closely with the nature spirits who tend the flowers and plants and all living things. The angel devas are kind of like the architects and the nature spirits are the builders. It all flows very smoothly, partly because they don't have free will to the extent that humans do, and partly because they are more in tune with the Divine Will.

Here are some examples of their order: The nature spirits work under the direction of an angel who has responsibility for a certain natural area—it may be a valley or a mountain peak or a forested area. The angel has a plan in tune with the overall plan of the earth and God. The angel passes his or her understanding on to the nature spirits, who in turn have their chain of command. So everything gets done in Divine Order.

In great reverence, I also would like to mention the great cosmic beings who are the overall leaders of the nature spirits—Beings of great intelligence and mastery of natural forces. They have names and personalities, and they are in male and female polarity. Oromasis and Diana are the leaders of the fiery salamanders. Aries and Thor are the leaders of the sylphs of the air. The gnomes are guided by Virgo and Pelleur. And the undines are led by, you may have guessed— Neptune and Luara. These great cosmic masters love and care for the nature spirits with the infinite love of God.

THE GNOMES

Now let's look closer at the four categories of nature spirits. The gnomes are the ones whom we have the most opportunity to work with. Anyone who has a garden, yard, house plants, or trees has a chance to work with gnomes on a daily basis. When I mention gnomes you may be picturing in your mind happy little elves in woodland clothes, or girlish fairies in pretty dresses, or rustic looking little men of traditional gnome appearance, but whatever charming, beautiful, quaint, or heroic image you may have of them, it's helpful to remember that they have personalities and they appreciate you giving them some regard and attention and even sincere praise. You may even think of them as innocent and beautiful and wise little children. Cicely Mary Barker used children as her models when she painted her lovely portraits of flower and plant fairies. You can also picture the gnomes as points of intelligent energy. You may not be able to see a brightly colored flower fairy, but you may see tiny flashes of light once in awhile.

The gnomes are naturally happy and fun-loving. They have no sense of good and evil as we do. They live for the beauty and creativity of God's handiwork. The gnome sees the inner lights—the currents of light in the plants—and the inner personalities of trees and perennial plants and responds to the inner workings of plants as she or he discharges the sunlight and cosmic energy into the plant.

The gnomes, elves and various kinds of fairies usually work as teams or groups. When their daily rounds are finished by the evening, they will often gather together to amuse themselves and share their joys.

Certain gnomes have been associated with gold. The folklore stories usually have the leprechauns or gnomes guarding or hoarding gold and some humans trying to figure out a way to get it from them. In actuality, the gnomes do work on the process of creating gold in the earth as well as all the other minerals, gems, and ores. Gold is symbolic of the Christ consciousness and carries the vibration of Christ. The gnomes would rather see the gold wind up in the possession of saintly people, so they try to hide it from greedy people. In this age the distribution of gold is out of balance. Much gold is controlled by people of unsaintly temperaments. In the golden ages of antiquity, gold was more fairly distributed. It's interesting to note that many families in India, a very spiritual country, place much importance in gold jewelry and other forms of gold.

The gnomes would be very happy to see the sparkling gems and valuable minerals distributed to deserving people. This is a universe of cause and effect and ultimate justice, consequently it will come out right in the end, but only God knows when. For now the underground gnomes just do their work of building the elements.

One reason nature spirits are so happy is because they don't live in an eat or be eaten world. They have no enemies, so they sing and dance and do all kinds of fun filled activities.

If good-natured human beings are having an outdoor ceremony or campfire sing along or any pleasant activity, the gnomes will gather around and watch and maybe mimic someone, or take part in the activity in their own way.

If you have a garden you can definitely invite the nature spirits to come and work with you. The nature spirits of the garden are more "domesticated" in a way, and are quite eager to work with "conscious" gardeners. More information on how to exactly work with the nature spirits will be given in the next chapter.

The reason elves are associated with Santa Claus, working at the North Pole to produce toys, is because elves can help manifest material objects. Jesus Christ could appear simultaneously in every home in the world, and the elves would help him manifest a gift for everyone. So, Santa Claus really could exist and get around to everyone on Christmas. The world isn't ready for that yet, but some day it may be.

Here is a message from one I call "the Golden Gnome": "I am a gnome from the gold mines. I have come to start another gold rush—from the golden treasury of the mind of Christ. This is the gold you want first—the gold of Christ consciousness. It is yours if you make the effort. Come one, come all."

UNDINES

Picture some beautiful mermaids with graceful figures, beguiling smiles, and a certain look of innocent seriousness or intent—but not sexy. Nature spirits are asexual although they may have the forms of men and women. The undines of freshwater lakes, rivers, and coastal ocean waters often take the forms of beautiful girls—and not half-fish either, although that is a form they may take from our thought projections.

The freshwater undines are usually one or two feet tall. They especially enjoy waterfalls because of the electric and magnetic energies generated there. They also like the quiet pools along rivers. At the seashore there are undines called "water babies" who love to frolic in the surf. They especially like it when the tide is coming. There seems to be extra cosmic currents and electric magnetism to work with during that time. When the tide goes out they take some time to rest. The water babies overflow with joy and try to spread their happiness to humans who play in the surf. When I used to live near the Pacific Ocean, I would ask the undines to body surf with me. I always felt refreshed and strengthened after playing in the surf with the water babies—beautiful little nature spirits of the sea. They love to ride along on surfboards, too. I don't think many surfers are aware of these little hitchhikers, but if you ride a surfboard or just play in the surf, you can ask them to join you, and you will get a good response.

Farther out from the shore, among coral reefs and kelp beds and other undersea habitats, all kinds of nature spirit activity is taking place as the ocean teems with life. The nature spirits have much to do in tending God's sea garden. They help to maintain the balance of nature under the sea. 'There are also past records of mankind to transmute—for example, the records of Atlantis have been transmuted during the past 12,000 years under the Atlantic Ocean. Water symbolizes the subconscious and the emotions. The undines work on those levels with us.

The undines are very devotional and love to sing the praises of God —the Creator of all. When their daily rounds are done, they will gather in their underwater grottos and celebrate with their own kind of special music that is in tune with the rhythm of the oceans.

And a few more words about the freshwater undines in case you haven't had much experience with the oceans. If you live near a river or lake or a pond, you may call on the undines to come out and play and work with you. They especially appreciate your efforts to help clean up lakes and river ways and groundwater pollution.

Whales and dolphins hold a special interest for undines. For one thing, certain advanced undines do take on the solid bodies of whales and dolphins and they can transmit extra portions of God's energy into the oceans and into the world. That's an extra reason to save the whales and work with the dolphins. There's no question that whales and dolphins have inspired mankind. Some of our popular movies such as "Free Willy" have been popular because of our connection with nature spirits.

Whenever a whale is killed, the undines gather around it and comfort it as it makes the transition to the next realm. The undines feel quite sad to lose a whale. In contrast to that, the undines rejoice greatly when people help to save the whales. A few years ago a whale was stuck in the ice floes in the Arctic Circle, through newspaper reports many people and countries as a whole responded to efforts to free that single whale.

It's beyond the scope of this book to go too much into the connection of animals and nature spirits. but through the guidelines in the next chapter you will understand the connection better.

Here is a message from a happy undine: "I am an undine of the water. Do you not like to take a shower or a bath or go for a swim? We would help you cleanse your emotional body. Feel your feelings of every glad emotion. Magnify them and feel how good you feel. It is like a shower—refreshing. Your other emotions will come and go, but do remember to take a 'joy' shower daily."

SYLPHS

We couldn't live without the sylphs of the air. The air is our most important sustainer of life. We can go without food, water, and heat for awhile, but only a few minutes without a breath of air. The sylphs are constantly washing and purifying the atmosphere, but we pollute it faster than they can clean it up. They are overburdened by the task. But as we learn how to reduce the air pollution, they will catch up again.

The sylphs are almost like angels, in fact they are evolving into angels. They are as beautiful as angels, come in many sizes, but usually about human size. Some of the high flying sylphs are very large. Sylphs are often associated with clouds—they play with clouds and push them around and into different shapes. Some people can suggest different shapes to cloud sylphs and they will try to oblige if the conditions are right. They love to arrange cloud patterns for sunrises and sunsets.

Just as the wind is associated with the Holy Spirit, so are the sylphs as they transmit the energies of God's Holy Spirit to us. The Holy Spirit is God's intelligent and loving vibration coursing through and sustaining all creation. The sylphs are in tune with that vibration or Holy Spirit and they step it down to make it comfortable for us and all life on the planet. The Holy Spirit is "the comforter" through the agency of the sylphs.

14

Just as air is in most things, so sylphs can interpenetrate the earth, sea and sky. The sylphs are the bringers of "prana", the life breath of the soul. As aspiring angels, they are most gracious and helpful to all of us. If you ask them, you will receive even more than the normal amount of help. This is part of a spiritual law: "Ask and you shall receive."

Special mention should be made of the storm spirits. These are a special class of sylphs that are active in storms, tornadoes, and hurricanes. They are not malevolent, but they do have a lot of fun helping to discharge all the energy in a storm. The weather patterns are not random. Angels of weather control the movements of big storms and they inform all the nature spirits of what needs to be done. It's a complicated subject as severe weather is linked to mass karma. The storm sylphs play out their roles as directed by the angels, and the angels try to preserve as much life as possible.

Sylphs are present at births and deaths of people. When you were born, there were sylphs in attendance. When you pass on, they will help you with the transition. That's another good reason to make friends of the sylphs.

Here is a message from a sunny sylph: "I am a sylph of the air. We would help you clean up and clean out your mind of the debris of unwanted habits and thoughts that you no longer need. Let the fresh winds blow them away. We will dispose of them. Replace them with every good thought and action you know of. You can do it with will power, which is given to you by God, and as such has the power of the universe behind it."

Now we come to the salamanders. They are probably the hardest to get to know as fire is dangerous and the misuse of fire and fiery salamanders has severe consequences. However, when you burn candles, especially altar candles, you can call for the presence of salamanders. They are very close to God because fire is light, and light is the gateway to God.

Cremation is the best way to dispose of dead bodies because the fiery salamanders will help free the soul from attachment to the body. In countries such as India where cremation is accepted as the best way to dispose of dead bodies, the salamanders are most happy to oblige. The sylphs join in the transition also as the smoke rises in the air. The gnomes can then use the ashes when they are spread on the ground, or if the ashes are put in a river, lake or ocean, the undines will use them.

In a country such as the United States, cremation is not widely practiced and the nature spirits have to deal with cemeteries full of dead bodies and lingering spirits. The nature spirits would be happier about it if we cremated dead bodies and instead created living memorials in our hearts—or just kept pictures or mementos in honor of the dead. The proper way to treat a dead body, if possible, is to put it on ice for two or three days, and then cremate it. Hold a separate memorial service for the still living spirit-soul of the person.

The salamanders oscillate in and out of the spiritual world, and as they do, they infuse the physical life on earth with spiritual fire. This is a work of immense but seemingly unspectacular importance. You hardly know it's being done. It's like our daily sunshine—we take it for granted. The spiritual fire does not burn, but it does purify.

The salamanders play a big role in transmuting and consuming the force fields of human hate, jealousy, greed, and other negative vibrations in the mass aura of the earth. This kind of work is very noticeable indeed because it is partly done with lightning bolts. At anytime during the day there are thunderstorms somewhere on earth. Lightning bolts unleash tremendous energy. The electric bolts carry the spiritual fire of the salamanders which help consume and transmute the negative force fields of human hate, etc. This is the salamanders' part. The angels of God do a lot of this kind of work.

Salamanders have always played a major role in forest fires. As you probably know, forest fires have a lot of good effects. They burn up the accumulated debris in the forest and then allow new cycles of growth to begin. As a forest fire begins to spread, more and more and larger salamanders come in to join the action. They are actually servants of mercy to the living things in the path of the fire. They help all the living trees, plants and animals doomed to destruction make the transition to the next realm of life.

Consciousness never dies. The nature spirits know this and they don't worry about death the way humans do. They do try to preserve life, but when so called death is inevitable, they take the necessary actions for the transition.

When a fire rages through human homes and buildings, it is a very serious matter to us, but it is the same role for the salamanders. Whether the fire got

17

started deliberately by someone or accidentally by nature or somebody's carelessness, the salamanders will be there as agents of mercy, even as they help burn things up. By the way, it is possible to control or influence the direction of fire by appealing to salamanders and sylphs of the wind and to the angels in charge of them and of course to God. A Saint of God could completely quench a fire by commanding the salamanders to withdraw.

Adepts can also create both a physical fire with mind power and their own electrical power and a spiritual fire that is called the "unfed flame." The "unfed flame" is a most holy spiritual fire tended by a high order of salamanders. In the best days of Atlantis they had a main "unfed flame" called the Maxin light. It burned by itself for centuries. It was used in major religious ceremonies. They also used it to cremate dead bodies. Anything put into this flame was immediately consumed and no trace of anything was left. The flame did not quiver at all. Such is the power entrusted to the highest order of salamanders.

Active volcanoes are another place where salamanders have burning roles to play. They can play and frolic and not be concerned with preserving life— until it comes time for an eruption. Volcanoes serve as another way for the nature spirits to help keep the balance of nature. Volcanic actions can destroy life, but they also build up mountains and spread volcanic ash which helps the ground become more fertile.

Here is a message from a fiery salamander: "I am a salamander of the fire. I come to set your love on fire. At the end of your earthly life you will look back and think I could have loved more. Why wait until then?

Think about it every day—How can I express more love today?"

THE BODY ELEMENTAL

Special mention should be made of our body elementals. Everyone has an elemental nature spirit to help the body function on the physical plane. The body elemental is your servant throughout life, and you in return are the body elemental's hope for eternal life. You can call on your body elemental to help you function, heal yourself, and to keep you healthy. They always do what they can to help you anyway, but it's a shame that they are hardly ever recognized or appreciated. The body elemental is not like your guardian angel, that is different, but he or she works with your guardian angel and your own holy Christ and God Self for your highest good.

Your body elemental helps you create and sustain your physical body from conception. He or she will stay with you from body to body in the rounds of reincarnation until you gain your freedom and establish your immortality. At that time your body elemental also gains his or her immortality.

Your body elemental will also help you work with all the other nature spirits. He or she will work with the salamanders on your etheric level; with the sylphs to aerate your mind so to speak; with the undines to cleanse your emotions; and with the gnomes to heal your physical body. By extension they will help you clean up the environment in the same way.

Special mention should also be made about the nature spirits of trees. Since trees are big, long-lived and play such an important role in the ecology of the planet, they deserve special recognition. Every tree has a tree spirit. As the trees grow, their spirits develop their personalities. You can feel the power of giant trees; the ones who have lived for hundreds of years. The ones who have been around humans have seen much of our history.

Tree spirits are busy during the day with all the functions of the tree, but during the night they may actually come out of the trees. They can't, however, venture very far from their trees. Forests at night can sometimes feel creepy to humans just because the tree spirits are out. The tree spirits talk to one another and exchange information. They also get help from tree fairies who are not attached to specific trees.

Tree spirits do not like to have their trees cut down, and consider it rude for humans to come into a forest and just start cutting without any warning or words of explanation. A tree spirit will accept the inevitable gracefully if someone gently explains why the tree is being cut down.

There is a Buddhist story about a fine, strong, old tree that a king was going to cut down in order to make a foundation for his palace. The tree spirit came to the king in a dream and appealed for mercy. The king insisted on cutting the tree, so the tree spirit asked if he would then cut the tree down branch by branch. The king asked why. The tree spirit explained that if the tree were felled in one mighty crash, it would injure or kill many of the baby trees growing around it. The king finally realized he was dealing with a very noble tree spirit and decided to spare the tree.

There are many accounts of so called "primitive people" who live close to nature refusing to cut down certain trees because they knew the tree spirit didn't want it to be cut down.

When I was younger I made the mistake of cutting down a tree that didn't want to be cut down. It was a tall pine tree. I thought I needed the wood for a building project. The tree spirit had a longer perspective and knew that I would never use the wood as I would be moving before long. I could hear an etheric scream when the tree crashed down. It shook me up, and I still regret cutting it down. You can't put a tree back up. I should balance this story with the time I refused to cut down a tree on a landscaping job because I knew the tree spirit didn't want it cut down. The owner of the land asked me to cut a jacaranda tree down. I just kept procrastinating that part of the job and never did cut it down.

If you really need to cut down a tree or trees, it would be a good idea to tell them at least a day ahead of time. Then perform a ceremony of some kind for them that honors their service. Then try to listen to the tree to know if it is willing to yield. When you go to sleep that night, remind yourself to remember your dreams in case the tree spirit comes to you with an appeal.

Tree farms are a different case. The tree spirits know the trees are being raised as a crop for human use—just like corn or whatever, but they do get to live longer than annual crops of course.

Some people have close relationships with trees. If you hug a tree, it will respond with friendly feelings.

Trees that are well cared for around homes radiate good feelings. If you honor a tree as another manifestation of the intelligence of God; if you treat it with dignity and respect, it will respond accordingly.

NATURE SPIRITS AND ANIMALS

This brings us to the next subject. We all know that animals respond to love and respect. The nature spirits help take care of animals. too, but it is beyond the scope of this book to go into detail about it. But there is one important subject that needs to be brought up when talking about helping the nature spirits clean up the environment—and that is slaughterhouses.

Slaughterhouses are places of mass killings of animals. Vibrations of incredible sadness and despair go out from slaughterhouses, and we need to do something about it. The case has already been made for the good sense and economics of a vegetarian or mostly vegetarian diet. This is up to each person however. It seems that most people who are serious about cleaning up the environment are cutting back on eating meat.

As far as the nature spirits are concerned, they have seen the inevitable fate of cows, chickens, and pigs being raised for slaughter. and they have "numbed" or even "dumbed" the animals marked for slaughter. That dumb or placid look of a cow grazing in a field may be due to the fact that nature spirits have clouded over its perception of its real condition and fate.

I have written a couple of poems about the conditions of cows. The first one shows the twist of how we can be sweet and cuddly with some animals, especially when they are just toy representatives like an Easter bunny, and on the other hand coldly send millions of animals to the slaughterhouses.

COWS CAN THINK

Cows can think; cows can blink:
Cows can a lot of water drink.
Isn't that funny like an Easter bunny?
Oh yes, the Easter bunny is funny and sunny.
He is a merry little fellow in Easter yellow.
But a cow I would describe as mellow.
Cows are subdued and languorous and the opposite of mercurious.
Although I realize that bulls can certainly get furious.
Cows munch grass all day, or, in winter, hay.
They move around slowly, and I seldom see them play.
They mostly seem dumb. How could one be your chum?
They chew and stare and are habitually mum.
Are they keeping secrets? Or silence about some regrets?
I wanted to know why they're not as light-hearted as, say, egrets.
I took an inner look at their hearts—open books.
The poor things, I wept to hear their story of the hooks.
We used to be so smart, but didn't know a cow had a heart.
We didn't know how they were killed and taken apart—
Their bodies hung on hooks, destined for thoughtless cooks,

Totally cut up and packaged in white for sanitary looks.
Oh yes, cows have thoughts, but they're tied off by knots;
So they won't have to think about the bloody end of their lots.
Can you imagine the slavery to intelligent beings full of knavery,
If they should keep you and think of you as tender and flavory?
And you were helpless and your situation seemed hopeless
For generations without end, would you be emotionless?
Oh yes, cows can think; cows can wink;
Cows should a lot of soma water drink.
Isn't that funny like the Easter bunny?
But when will their resurrection come up sunny?

SOME COWS REFUSE SLAUGHTER

Gliding over the farms, far from the daily battle,
Overseeing the pastures and fields green with life
On pleasing hills with barbed wire fences making boundaries,
I dream of free birds flying and captive cattle
Munching herbs, unaware of their future shock, future strife.
Unaware that green fields give way to red factories.
Unaware that yonder man riding stoutly in the saddle
Comes to drive them deftly to the gates of perdition;
Comes to routinely drive them to their utter destruction.

Here he comes, not giving their group soul a single
thought.
Here he is. Whoa, woe! Whoa, woe! Whoa, woe!
Oh Jesus, he's gonna kill my father and mother!
But look! A berserk Brahma bull charges in a wild
run.
He' s going straight at the man, the false friend, the
foe.
He's caught him by surprise. Woe big brother!
The man is knocked off the horse; the rebellion has
begun.
Scatter! No regroup. Head for the hills! What about
the fences?
Oh, the fences! We forgot, cows can't make it past
them.
The barbed wire will hurt. They are limited to their
senses.
What now? The man will recover every last one of
them.
The dream is over; sixty billion served, one billion
dead,
And here I sit, dumbly-numbly crying in bed.
Before I again take leave of my five senses,
I must go take down those barbed wire fences.

NATURE SPIRITS AND RELIGION

The tribes of people who still live close to the earth
have a long history of relating to nature spirits, and
they give various measures of importance to them in
their contexts of religious beliefs. When I lived in
Borneo, I learned that the "Rice Spirit" was important
to the tribes who grew a lot of rice. The "Rice Spirit"
was and is the angel deva in charge of rice, so they

were appealing to a real spirit who did respond to them, and the fairies of the rice angel did their work also on behalf of the tribal people.

The angels and nature spirits will try to work for anyone who calls on them for help, but if you call on them in the name of Jesus Christ, Bhagavan Krishna, Gautama Buddha, or any other great person who is one with God, you will get a better response; or you may call on them in the name of your own "I am" God presence and "Holy Christ Self". Or you may call on them directly in the name of our Father-Mother God. It depends on your personal religious beliefs, but the nature spirits will understand your feelings of reverence because they also have a great reverence for God and the saints of God. They simply adore Jesus Christ, Buddha, Krishna, and others who have manifested the love of God on earth.

So the nature spirits are not to be worshipped or propitiated in a superstitious way. They are not above humans, but they would love to join you in singing the praises of God and His/Her Divine emissaries. You can invite nature spirits to join you in any religious service that honors God and the sons and daughters of God.

A few words of clarification should be written here about some of the scary type of stories handed down from European folk tales. They do not really apply to the vast majority of nature spirits. There have been people on the negative side of life who have enslaved nature spirits, and used them for evil purposes. Part of your work can be to help set such nature spirits free from negative influences of people with bad intentions. You can do this by praying for them.

Wood elf dedicating his energies

27

Undine mermaid playing with dolphins

Shy sylph sprites waiting to be introduced

Boyish salamander showing mastery of fire

CHAPTER TWO

"Oh, then, soul most beautiful among all creatures, so anxious to know the dwelling place of your Beloved that you may go in quest of Him and be united with Him, and now we are telling you that you yourself are his dwelling...his secret chamber and hiding place."

-St. John of the Cross
The Spiritual Canticle

YOUR CONSCIOUS COOPERATION

Now we come to the "how to help" part of the book. This is a chance for you to adjust your daily awareness to the inclusion of the presence of friendly nature spirits in your environment. You can do it if you want to strongly enough because the same Spirit that animates the nature spirits also enlivens you. We're all one in the circle of life. God is the point of contact for any other part of life.

EXPERIMENTS IN TRUTH

Mahatma Gandhi entitled his autobiography "Experiments in Truth." I always thought that would be a good title for anybody's life story who is willing to have an open mind and tries to find out what life is all about. So this conscious cooperation between you and the nature spirits is an experiment in finding out the truth about life—your life and the life around you.

Keep a notebook. Be systematic if you will. Here are some of the guidelines to help you in this radiant endeavor.

31

(A) HAVE FAITH IN YOURSELF

Most people seem to believe in God, and angels, and many also believe in the existence of nature spirits, but the problem seems to be that many people have trouble believing in themselves and that God actually lives within each one of us. The concept that we are all sinners cut off from any direct contact with God doesn't do much for self-esteem.

So one of the first steps is to establish that firm belief in your own "God Self." This is different from a faith in your own human ego. You may have all sorts of wonderful abilities and talents, but if you attribute them to your own ego—well, we all know pride goes before a fall. But if you have that great faith that you are part of the Creator of the universe, and that you have all kinds of amazing abilities because of your identity with God, then you are well on your way to wonderful adventures.

(B) THE IMPORTANCE OF HUMILITY

If you approach nature spirits—or people, with a superior attitude, you are closing off open communication. No one, no thing likes to be treated as inferior. If you think your dog, cat, goldfish, or even your rosebush is inferior to you, you may need to think deeper about that. Your human life may be more economically valuable. You may be more intelligent, and your life may be more worthwhile to society, and if you had to choose between your life and a dog's life, you would rightfully choose your own. However, since all life comes from one ultimate source, and we're all interrelated and interdependent in the one life of God, why think of yourself as either superior or inferior? You're just you—the great and glorious You; and so is every one else. You might be surprised at the wisdom of a goldfish if you could hear the voice of God coming through it. So you might as well be humble about your own greatness.

God is the ultimate in humility. God remains hidden and does everything, knows everything, and is the greatest person of all, yet you hardly know He or She is around. God is the great Tao. When you approach the nature spirits with true humility they will pick up your mental attitude. Humble people are inwardly strong. Cultivate humility in yourself, and it will open up lines of communication. You may receive the wisdom of God from anywhere, anyone.

(C) LIVE OUT OF A PURE HEART WITH PURE MOTIVES

The love of God is the best motive for doing anything. Since "God" has different meanings for different people, I will explain what I mean by this. We may have all kinds of different motives for our actions, but if you analyze them, you will come down to the fact that you want to be happy. Even when people do hurtful actions, it's because they want something that will make them feel better or happier. A bank robber wants money so he can buy something that will make him happy. A girl wants a boy's attention because that will make her happy. The examples are endless.

When you realize that happiness is what you really want, and that all forms of worldly happiness will eventually fade, then you may finally realize that the only source of true and everlasting, ever-new happiness is God.

This will simplify your motives and simplify your life. Your heart will become more pure because you will realize that being kind, generous, considerate, and being your real God Self is what brings you the most happiness. Your happiness producing actions will bring more happiness into your life. and you will naturally do what is right. Of course it isn't that easy, is it?   Nevertheless, if your motive is to love God, then that happiness will spring up from within you.

God may be thought of as personal or impersonal, male or female, or as Truth, Beauty, Love, Bliss, Cosmic Intelligence, the Divine Mind or all of the above and more. However you think of God, it's beneficial to have a personal and intimate relationship with your concept of God. Your understanding will grow and grow.

The nature spirits are already happy and they will welcome you to the club. If a gloomy person walks into their gardens, forests, lakes, or wherever, they may try to cheer him up, but they love it when a happy person comes around.

If you are temporarily in distress, feeling sad or angry about something, you can be consoled by the angels and nature spirits by going for a walk in the woods, by the seashore, in the mountains, or even a city park. You can walk and talk with God, Jesus, Buddha or whoever your true friend is, and the angels and nature spirits will be there to help you too, if you can call on them in the name of God.

If you're really having heavy problems with addictions, abuse, mental instability, relationships and so on, then you probably need some professional help or some kind of help from your fellow human beings. I just want to remind you that you have lots of unseen help, and even more if you ask for it because angels don't interfere with your free will.

To solve your problems you must come back to your own motives, attitudes, and will power.

(D) HAVE MUTUAL RESPECT, COURTESY, AND APPRECIATION

Respect breeds respect. Courtesy breeds more courtesy. Appreciation breeds more appreciation. I'm sure you have noticed that. This is important in approaching the nature spirits. They like to have the respect that "nature knows what it is doing"—even when it is just growing weeds in a vacant lot. You can give audible or silent appreciation to the work of the nature spirits every day. They're at work in the sky, in the fields, in the water, in the fires of all kinds. They will in turn notice you and what you're doing, even if you don't think you're doing much. Anybody can pray, and prayer is a form of energy that goes out to the world—and angels use that energy under the direction of God and pass some of it on to the nature spirits to work with.

(E) HAVE CHILD-LIKE INNOCENCE

Children sometimes see angels and fairies. I love to see the innocence of children. Most of us seem to lose that innocence as we grow older, but it can be regained. Hanging around small children can help you, if you're willing to learn from them. Unfortunately, television programs, the adult advertisements on TV, and many popular movies that even small children seem to know about has speeded up the loss of innocence in children.

This is actually a very serious matter because television has the effect of reducing children's inner creativity. A strong case has already been made for limiting television time for children and adults; so I won't go into it here. My concern is how to cultivate that innocence. What is it really? I think it is the ability to see with fresh eyes, not jaded by too much worldly experience. It's a belief in the inherent purity and rightness of life. It's a simple faith in the goodness of life and the protection of an over-all Spirit—God.

The following technique is a way to regain some of that innocence.

(F) TRY THE "CLEAN SLATE" METHOD

Every day is new. Every day is a new opportunity to expand your consciousness, increase your wisdom and love, The past is in the record books, and you want to keep your best and most useful memories, but every day is a "clean slate." If you wake up with the attitude that you still have much to learn; then you will be open to new thoughts and ideas.

How well do you really know your spouse, brother, sister, co-workers, friends, your dog, or your rosebush? You may have stereotyped them or fit them into your own pre-conceived notions. My point is to awaken your mind to all sorts of new possibilities.

It's good to be aware of your pre-conceived notions and to be on guard against the influence of "opinion makers" such as newscasters, editorial writers and columnists, politicians, advertisers, movies, and the hidden manipulators of common fears and prejudices.

In regard to nature spirits, the "clean slate" method is a good way to rid yourself of the old stories of elves, gnomes, fairies, etc., most of which don't give an accurate picture at all. Some of the stories may have originally had some basis in fact, but over the mists of time, the stories have changed. Most people probably never took those stories seriously anyway. The morals of the stories may be true, but not the facts. The nature spirits work in the "eternal now."

You can get back some of the innocence of early childhood if you can daily clear your mind of the jaded influences of the world and live to experience the joys of God, the angels, and nature spirits.

(G) USE POSITIVE DECREES

Along with clearing your mind of limited and wrong ideas, it's good to fill your mind with positive thoughts and mental and verbal decrees. Your thoughts and decrees have the power to change things. God is the original decreer. When He said "Let there be light," He used His words and visualization of what light is. Since we are part of God, our thoughts and words have strong effects. This is why the Bible and other scriptures counsel us to avoid slander and harsh words and to speak kindly and compassionately to one another.

The angels and nature spirits enjoy gentle and kindly speech. On the other hand they recoil or even withdraw when harsh and hurtful words are spoken. Cussing and cursings are a real burden to the nature spirits. All those negative words and thoughts coalesce into negative energy fields that have to be transmuted. It's sad to hear even young children repeating the cursings of adults.

You can consciously help create positive energy fields by thinking good thoughts and verbally saying affirmations and decrees. This can become a daily and systematic practice. You can start, end, and intersperse your days with affirmations and decrees. I have listed resources at the end of this book in case you need some.

The verbal decrees can be very simple. You don't have to be eloquent. The heart quality of love is what matters most. You can say something simple like, "In the name of God, let there be more light." Or, "Let there be more love in the world." Or you can be more specific, "I am a kind person." Any statement that starts with "I am" is very powerful because "I AM" is a name of God. It's important to preface your decrees by saying something to the effect of "In the name of my own God presence and holy Christ Self." This gives added weight and effect to your decrees. You can invite angels and the omnipresent saints of God to reinforce your decrees. And you can invite the nature spirits to decree with you.

By saying decrees and affirmations you have thus created some positive energy for the world. You can seal this energy to be used only for good by saying, "Let these decrees be sealed in the holy light, love, and will of God." This protects your energy from the misuse by human will power, which can go astray even with good intentions.

Along with consciously using positive affirmations and decrees, it's good to work on your sub-conscious decrees. Your conscious mind may be saying one thing and your sub-conscious mind might be sabotaging your efforts. Even now it might be saying something like, "This fairy stuff is nonsense." A lot of doubts and fears may lurk in the sub-conscious mind. It's good to remember that everything in your sub-conscious mind can be changed or transmuted or at least analyzed once it is brought to the surface.

J. Allan Boone tells a marvelous story in his book, *Kinship With All Life*, about his little friend "Freddie" the fly. Through positive mental imaging and purifying his thoughts and motives he was able to make a friend out of a common housefly. When people with a bad attitude toward flies came around to visit Mr. Boone, Freddie would not go near them, even when they tried to coax him to come. Mr. Boone concluded that Freddie intuitively knew that the people sub-consciously disliked flies, whereas Mr. Boone was able to clear out of his sub-conscious the dislike for flies. Then he was able to communicate with Freddie on the basis of their commonality—their connection to God.

This story illustrates what we need to realize—that God is in us and all around us in visible and invisible life. Our conscious minds can accept that as truth, but until we know it within every cell of our bodies and throughout our sub-conscious and super-conscious minds, we will just be "on the path" to knowledge. Meanwhile, if we make positive mental and verbal decrees every day, we will be contributing to the enlightenment of all life on earth.

(H) USE BEAUTIFUL. MUSIC

Music is very important in establishing rapport with the nature spirits. They love to sing and dance and play music that relates to and praises God in some way—because God is joy, bliss, love, truth, beauty, and every good quality.

As you may have guessed, this puts them at odds against a lot of contemporary music that is full of degrading language, sexual innuendoes, discordant sounds, and downright violence.

Music is built into the fabric of creation. In fact musical rhythms sustain creation; so it is very important that our music harmonizes with the music of the spheres.

Experiments have shown the effects of various types of music on plants and animals. They respond much better to music such as Strauss Waltz's, pieces by Bach, Vivaldi, Mozart, and other classical composers. Indian ragas and bhajans also have a good influence on plants and animals.

In contrast, hard rock, heavy metal, blues, and jazz have a depressing effect on plants and animals. The plants don't grow much or they grow away from the music. Cows give less milk So you can infer that the nature spirits don't like that kind of music either.

This may be a controversial point for people who like that kind of music, especially jazz aficionados. Jazz is hard to define, but the pulsation and syncopation are very pronounced. Syncopation places the accent on the off-beat in 4/4 time and thus disrupts the evenness of the rhythm. The effect is not to enlighten but to drive the human energy toward sensuality.

Music releases into the material world a fundamental superphysical energy that affects everything. Music has the power to lift us up or drag us down. It affects the very atoms of creation—our building blocks. I offer no final words on the subject, but it is definitely worth thinking about if you're serious about helping to clean up the environment.

All day and night long music is going out to the world through radio stations. Rock, jazz, and country-western music dominate the air waves. They are making musical decrees that affect life on this planet. There's usually only one classical music radio station per city, and not all classical music has positive effects. Religious music stations help somewhat with their musical programs, but I would like to see a radio station dedicated to playing all the kinds of music that is good for our environment, and thus naturally enjoyable to the nature spirits.

Here are a few suggestions on music for the different types of nature spirits. For fire: Beethoven's symphonies Nos. 5 and 9. Verdi's Grand March from Aida, Sibelius's Finlandia, Wagner's Ride of the Valkyries, and Rachmaninoff's piano concertos Nos. 2 and 3. For earth: Massanet's Meditation (from Thais), Brahm's' symphony No. 3, and Beethoven's symphony No. 6. For air: Mozart's Horn concerto, Shankar's Indian ragas, Tibetan bells, and Elgar's Enigma variations. For water: Handel's water music, Strauss's Blue Danube waltz, Mahler's symphonies Nos. 4 and 6. A lot more music is pleasing to the nature spirits.

Some of the "new age" music is very much in tune with nature. Please see the resources at the end of the book for more information on music.

(I) FEEL AND EXPRESS GRATITUDE

If you make a conscious effort to feel and express gratitude about every good thing in your life, you're bound to feel more joy. Some people even feel gratitude for setbacks and problems because such things help them to grow. That's important because if you curse your "bad luck" you usually get more bad luck.

In regards to the nature spirits, you can express your gratitude to them every day. You can thank the sylphs for purifying the air and for making beautiful sunsets and for all the other work they do.

Every time you eat you can thank the gnomes for their part in growing food. In fact, you can thank them for all the bounty of the earth. If you own gems, you can thank them for their role in forming gems in the earth. You can thank them for all the materials in your house.

You can thank the undines for all the uses of water in your life, and the salamanders for the uses of fire and electricity in your life.

Such gratitude is real, and it is received by the angels and nature spirits, and they respond just as you probably would—they want to do even more. That doesn't make it your motive. The spirit of gratitude helps everyone feel better, and we naturally want to keep it flowing.

This works in all areas of your life. Even if you eat a hamburger at a fast food restaurant, you can thank the cow that gave its life for you. How many people do you suppose do that? You may thank God for your food and that would cover everything, but it's good to remember everyone else involved sometimes.

(J) REALIZE THE FLUIDITY AND FLEXIBILITY OF NATURE

In working with nature spirits, it's good to think about how the physical forms on this earth are constantly changing. Forms come and go, but the life consciousness is always present. We may get attached to people, animals, trees, or whatever, and we can love the physical forms as well as the inner life, but love is also involved in the release of physical forms.

The nature spirits realize this and do not become attached to the physical forms, yet they love the physical forms because they help to build and grow the natural forms of the earth. It's a good lesson to remember.

(K) THE IMPORTANCE OF COURAGE

It takes courage to express your belief in nature spirits—not necessarily in angels or God, but if you mention fairies, gnomes, or mermaids in a serious way, you may be subject to ridicule, especially among people who have little connection with nature or who are just blind to all the unseen forces around us. Even people who are close to nature, such as modern farmers, may laugh at the notion of nature spirits that are real. The traditional notions of nature spirits hamper people from taking them seriously.

It also takes courage to work with nature spirits because there is so much that is unknown, and people are afraid of the unknown. Suppose a little wood elf did pop out from behind a tree. Could you handle it? Actually, that's not likely to happen, but it does take courage to open your consciousness to the presence of nature spirits.

(L) MEDITATION

In order to become inwardly quiet so that you can listen to the voices of nature, you need to have some kind of meditation technique. You may have your own way of calming your mind, but if you don't, it's good to find someone to teach you or a book to learn from. Meditation is a religious practice—all the religions have some meditation techniques. "Be still and know that I am God." is a Bible verse often quoted in this regard.

In working with nature spirits you're actually working with God, so the more you can listen to God through meditation, the more you can be in tune with nature spirits. What you're doing is working with God, with the angels, with the nature spirits, and with the saints of God in cleaning up the environment.

(M) THE IMPORTANCE OF PRAYER

Many fine books have been written about the efficacy of prayers. Prayer is certainly a prime activity in working with nature spirits. You can pray for them because of all the work they do in transmuting the negative energies of mankind. And you can invite them to pray with you about every situation that you may want to pray about.

Your own heart can be an altar for the nature spirits, for you have something they do not have—the three-fold flame in your spiritual heart. Although nature spirits are in tune with the inner workings of nature, they are not endowed with all the spiritual faculties of mankind. We may be ignorant of many things, but when a person fully develops his or her human and divine potential, that person can do all kinds of "miraculous" work that exceeds what nature spirits are capable of doing.

So when you pray for the nature spirits, you magnetize their presence. You can say a simple prayer such as "In the name of Christ (or Krishna), I ask for the healing of all elemental life—sylphs, gnomes, salamanders, and undines." Or you could say a variation on the rosary, "Hail Mary, full of grace, the Lord is with thee. Blessed art thou among women and blessed is the fruit of thy womb, Jesus. Holy Mary, mother of God, pray for all elemental life of fire, air, water, and earth."

Mankind has placed a real burden on elemental life, so it is our duty to give intercessory prayer on their behalf. They in turn can help us more. For example, when a hurricane, tornado, or other violent weather is coming, you can pray for the mitigation of serious effects. Your prayers will enable the angels and nature spirits to protect more life. Prayer can also change dire prophecies. We have heard much about coming earth changes. Prayer can do much to change future prospects. The nature spirits will be with you for a better world.

(N) HAVE A GOOD DIET

A good diet is essential in maintaining your body and mind. A vegetarian or near vegetarian diet is conducive to cultivating a connection with the nature spirits. Diet is such an individual matter though; so I hesitate to make any recommendations. This is a matter which everyone needs to experiment with themselves. My point is to take the subject of diet and nutrition seriously.

If you have a vegetable garden and invite the nature spirits to help you grow the vegetables, those vegetables will actually be laden with more than the usual amount and quality of vitamins and minerals because of the extra vitality given to them by the nature spirits.

(O) GO BEYOND THE FIVE SENSES

Within every object which the senses can identify is the "spiritual fact" functioning in all its completeness and perfection. Within a tree is the perfect idea of the tree as conceived by God. If you train your mind to look for the "perfect presence within everything, you will appreciate the uniqueness and preciousness of every form. You will become more aware of the abilities of plants and animals to adapt to life, and you will get more insights into the work of the nature spirits.

Scientists use their five senses and all kinds of ingenious instruments, machines, and methods for delving into the secrets of nature, but I would guess that a lot of it is done without regard to the nature spirits. The current research into DNA and gene-splicing is fraught with danger. Mother Nature has an awesome power that scientists can't always handle. The scientists who go beyond reliance on the five senses are the ones who will be able to get real insight into the workings of nature.

Within our present scientific framework, you won't be able to prove the existence of gnomes, angels, or even God, but I do give credit to scientists for discovering and using many of the unseen forces and energies around us, such as radio waves, magnetism, and so on.

If you practice a scientific method of meditation, you will be able to go beyond the five senses. In silent meditation you can close down the "five sense telephones" and let your spiritual intuition rise to the top. Scientific meditation is best done with a mentor, guru, or qualified teacher. Personally I recommend Paramahansa Yogananda, author of the spiritual classic *Autobiography of a Yogi*. He has left a detailed method of scientific meditation, available from Self-Realization Fellowship. Their address is in the list of resources.

(P) KINESIOLOGY

Kinesiology is a method you can use with nature spirits. It is a method of testing your muscle strength in relation to a question, or food, music, pictures—anything that affects you. The idea is to see if something makes you stronger or weaker—thus indicating a negative or positive response, or a yes or no answer. You can use different muscles, but to do it without the help of someone else, the finger muscles are the best ones to use.

If you're right handed, put the thumb and little finger of your left hand together; put your right thumb and index finger together in the apex of the circle made by your left thumb and little finger, then ask questions that have simple yes or no answers. You can ask the questions of your own higher Self.. Some examples of questions: "In the name of my mighty I AM presence and holy Christ Self, should I plant tomatoes in this area?" Or, "Should I put bone meal in the garden?" Then you apply pressure on your left thumb and little finger with your right thumb and index finger—trying to push them apart. If you can't push them apart, it indicates a "yes" answer because your muscles stay strong. This takes some practice. You might begin with questions that you already know the answer to, such as, "Is my name —"? Your body elemental will help you with this. Consult a book on kinesiology for more details.

I have put this idea of kinesiology near the end of the "how to" chapter because it's a good idea to practice the other suggestions first. They will give you a good foundation to work on.

(Q) TRY TO SEE THINGS FROM A NATURE SPIRIT'S VIEWPOINT

I offer the following poems as a way of seeing into the lives of trees and plants and thus into the work of nature spirits, but there is much more to imagine. remember, the nature spirits are involved in the natural processes of nature—absorption, assimilation, discharge, transmutation, and transmittal. They bring more vitality to everything they touch..

RETURN OF THE NATURE SPIRITS

Among the shadeless trees and bitter streams
he played as a lonely child
Ignorant of why madmen shattered the Motherland and her
people
Until he met, deep in the broken forest,
a strange man, half-wild,
Who told him of dark forces that were extremely powerful,
And for vivid proof, he showed him,
after tapping him by the heart,
The hunched up existence of gnomes and elves in seeming
defeat
Looking bent, bowed, and grim; their diligent work
being torn apart.
For they were, (as explained to him), taking on
mankind's karmic load
In order to hold the world's balance
lest greater cataclysm fall.
They only wanted to love, help, and serve
in their own charming mode,
But too many humans wanted power, gain, and gold—
some even wanted "all."
After viewing the mournful scene, the little boy
began to cry.

And through his tears and his awe said, "Please tell me
what to do and why."
The youthful years passed, the lessons were learned.
The boy became a man,
Learned about his work in the world, found his mate
and acquired some land.
They followed the meek wisdom of Nature's way
and were astounded;
Their land flourished everywhere—in field, forest,
garden and orchard.
Streams ran pure, wild flowers went berserk,
wild animals abounded.
From the hills that half-wild man came again,
clothed as a shepherd.
He told them of others making a comeback,
then opened their eyes:
Suddenly—a scene of gnomes, elves, and fairies
working gleefully,
Singing, dancing, and chanting and carrying on
so cheerfully.
The man boy cried again—for joy, his "eye" seeing
through God's disguise.

THE GODWOOD TREE

I am in God, I am in wood. I am the Godwood tree
I dwell in the forests among my brethren.
You could, if you would, experience me.
Put aside your wooden facts. Be willow children
And come inside my trunk. Anchor your feet in my roots.
Feel the grasp I have in the earth, feel the strong hold.
Feel the spread, the growth, the feeding of my roots.
Now stretch your arms into my branches. Be bold!
Thrust yourself into every branch, twig, and bud.
My sap is rising. My buds are swelling.
Springtime is coming. Mingle in my sap your blood
And live the rebirth of a tree in this dwelling.
Let us prepare just as a royal bride prepares.
The snow has melted; the days are warmer and longer.
The squirrels are stirring; bears are leaving their lairs;

The Spirit of spring is moving and becoming stronger.
Feel my blossoms now as they open in a spray of whiteness.
I'm covered with white flowers, slightly tinged with pink.
The bees, insects, and people are attracted by my brightness.
Sense my essential oneness with all life, deep as you can think
Now feel my light green leaves as they slowly emerge
To form their veiny network in a set pattern.
Each one I know. All together we get a surge
Of growth as the sun shines in and the cycles turn
Toward full summer. My dear blossoms fade and drop
And my bright, little red berries begin to grow.
Hundreds of birds will harvest my red berry crop
Later on in Autumn and during winter snow.
But now the summer heat builds up the thunderheads
Which release the cooling showers of glancing rain,
And I drink water with my roots under stream beds.
I'm satisfied and full till summer begins to wane.
Water becomes scarce for awhile in the August drought.
Do you feel my thirst as my leaves begin to tire?
I feel droopy and ready for a turnabout.
The rain comes again and averts a forest fire.
A cold snap shivers my sap; it wants to withdraw.
All of me wants to withdraw. My leaves turn red-brown.
We'll make a grand exit that leaves humans in awe
A glorious Autumn until our leaves fall down.
So they fall: merrily, merrily, merrily.
Life is a dream; and during the long winter season,
In the middle of cold and snow, I dream of being a tree
Because that's what I am—my natural reason.
for the birds I have left bare branches and berries
While I go inward to be with the tree fairies.
I am the Godwood tree, misnamed the dogwood tree.
If they have misnamed you, assert your Godliness.
Then you and I and all who live for loveliness
Will waken some Spring day and blossom in our unity

THE CUCUMBER PLANT

In May, when the fluffy garden soil warmed my toes,
I planted my cucumber seeds in careful rows—
Smooth and whitish seeds that contained originality,
Little gems that would sprout forth green vitality
While spreading rootlets into the compost rich soil
To absorb vital elements—this being the plant's toil.
I tucked each one into its comfortable, earthy home,
Chanting the sacred mantras of the Divine .Mother with Om,
And invoking the aid of elemental beings in number
Along with angel devas who are intimate with cucumber.
They would need a proper mixture of heat, water,
Air, earth, and (without skepticism) something called ether.
After planting the cucumber seeds, I planted their chums.
Those merry, round-faced, happy-go-wacky
flowers—nasturtiums,
And I prayed that the dreaded cucumber beetle pest
Would not come here looking for a home to infest.
Within five days, after a soaking good rain at night,
Rows and rows of cucumber sprouts pushed into the light.
Fresh and fragile looking as all new-born living things,
They eagerly drank in the sunshine and air as in first time
flings.
Then they began forming big leaves and long stems,
Their baby tendrils searched for something to cling to, (hems?)
And gradually found my framework of criss-crossed bamboo
poles.
By the end of June they had grown beyond all my controls
And spread themselves over and past their allotted space.
magically they put out little yellow flowers apace
That bees obligingly came to take pollen from and fertilize.
After the flowers fell away, tiny cucumbers began to rise.
They just appeared. I don't know how—but whee!
Eventually those cucumbers would get inside of me,
But for now I wanted to get inside a cucumber;
So, at the juncture of stem and fruit, I slipped in at slumber.
I felt very white and moist and pleasantly cool.
I felt the pattern and structure of inherent rule,
And l felt juices—strong, intelligent, determined juices

Full of various elements and vitamins pressing into me—ooooh juices!
I began to grow long to accommodate the elemental compounds
At the same time I increased my girth, reaching my bounds.
Long and well-rounded—not fat and funny or skinny and sickly,
I became quite symmetrical, my skin was green and smooth—not prickly.
I was, in truth, a very good-looking cucumber specimen.
Inside I felt something entirely new to me, something of women:
Seeds forming in my middle, a hundred of them, more or less,
Encased in a Jell-O-like substance that sustained the process.
I was a mother! With a hundred seed children in me.
Oh I wanted to live and let my seeds reach maturity.
Then I felt my connection with the other ladies of the vine.
All of we cucumbers, laying in shade or hanging in the sunshine,
Felt the same basic desire to reproduce our kind.
But a few were troubled and deeply in a bind,
For insects had sucked life-giving juices from their stems,
And they were not getting enough nutrients into their systems.

I became aware of an intricate network of communication.
The whole garden was full of chatter, mostly in jubilation.
It was a heady experience until suddenly it happened:
I was picked! Severed from the vine. I was, gulp, de-gardened!
By myself! I almost forgot; I am not a cucumber,
But it was a delicious experience inside of her.
Here was the cucumber in my hands. What should I do?
I ate it. Clean and crisp, with thanks to you know who.
Many other cucumbers followed that one to the kitchen,
But I left some to fully ripen their seeds to fruition
For I learned an intimate, endearing and special reason
To leave some mature cucumber seeds for the next season.

THE DIVER'S WORLD

Diving into the world beneath the coral sea
the diver brushes past the purple fridmani
And sees two eagle rays gliding through the shallows
Riding an undersea wind, moving like dark shadows.
Further down he sees and undulating sea slug
and a scorpion fish with a smug ugly mug.
Tiny shrimp on crimson steeds ride by him.
Next, small plaid-clad hawkfish, following every whim,
Dart by. Reaching bottom, he disturbs a ballet—
Sea cucumbers in a graceful courtship display.
In contrast, a prickly sea urchin fights against
A triggerfish who seems to be rather incensed.
meanwhile, a crocodile fish lies in wait for food.
His softly smiling jaws feigning a benign mood.
Nearby, a hump-back ungainly anglerfish fishes
Among pink tube sponges, scaring the near misses.
Moving on, the diver avoids a pointy rock—
That moves! — a stone fish that would give a painful shock
From its venomous fins. Let the diver beware!
There are many strange creatures that may not play fair.
And then barracuda! — the wolfpack of the reef,
Long-nosed and needle-teethed, bringing instant grief,
Come to threaten him, but the encounter is brief
As they turn away, much to the diver's relief.
Wishing to avoid any domain-type quarrel
He ascends to inspect the polyps of soft coral
Which capture the plankton with tiny tentacles.
Moving upward still, he sees crabs and barnacles.
Then he surfaces again to the world we know
And thinks about the watery world just below—
Worlds undreamed of by creatures of air and land.
How many more worlds are there undreamed of by man?

CHAPTER 3

CONCLUSION

HOW WILL ALL THIS HELP?

"Nature, take thy freedom! Spirits of nature, Rejoice!
For the impositions of mankind shall not rest upon thee longer than the law itself will allow. And the time of thy deliverance is at hand"

-El Morya

The nature spirits love you—the God potential in you. They love the earth. They want us to be happy. They are happy- even ecstatic.

If we improve ourselves, we will improve the world. If we clean out the toxins in ourselves, we automatically improve the world. The "How to" suggestions are good for relating to everyone as well as to the nature spirits.

All life responds to kindness. It will come back to you. Even if you never see a gnome or sylph or any nature spirit (but you probably will see their points of light, if not their ethereal bodies), you will be helping them by following these suggestions, and they will be grateful to you.

Most of us lead busy lives with a lot of things to think about. We're busy relating to people we can see and to all the physical, tangible things of the earth, so you may not have much time to relate to invisible beings such as angels and nature spirits, nevertheless even a few moments of attention will have some effects. Give a short prayer or acknowledgment, or even a "Good morning, God bless you today angels and nature spirits".

If you're really into this, you can do a lot more, of course. There are a lot of programs now for kids and adults to help with cleaning up our environment. If you're involved in any of these programs, such as a river or lake cleanup—or recycling efforts or political action, you can enlist the support of the nature spirits. They have a tremendous ability to have fun. "Be happy—don't worry" is probably one of their slogans. Life is never dull or boring for them. They live for beauty.

I would like to publish a longer, more detailed book about the nature spirits. If you have stories to share, please send them to me at the publisher's address. If you can share this information with children, it would be of great benefit to them and the nature spirits. I would also like to reach teenagers with this information, but I'm afraid they will not like the section on music. This is most unfortunate. So many teenagers seem to favor music of passion and rebellion, and by this they distance themselves from the angels of harmony and true love. Angelic music could help lift them out of their confusion. I do know many teenagers like uplifting music, and maybe if they knew the true effects of different kinds of music, they would make spiritually-oriented music the predominate music heard over the airwaves.

SUMMARY

Here is a summary of how you can help the nature spirits clean up the environment: (1) Have faith in your own God Self—that you have the ability to make the connection. (2) Stay humble with your power—it comes from God, and it is an attractive quality. (3) Keep your motives pure—the best way to do that is to act in the love of God. The nature spirits respect that. (4) Have respect and appreciation for the nature spirits and their handiwork. (5) Cultivate childlike innocence; the nature spirits love the innocence of children. (6) Have an open mind about the unseen forces around us. There may be many angels and nature spirits ready to help you if you would only ask them to. (7) Use positive decrees. Angels and nature spirits respond to your affirmations and calls to make conditions better. (8) Use beautiful music. Music makes powerful vibrations. Nature spirits like music that is positive and uplifting. You can play music especially for them and invite them to listen. (9) Feel and express your gratitude for life. The nature spirits think life is wonderful, even though the earth is in danger. Gratitude helps us to not take things for granted, and it brings more good things into our lives. (10) Realize that the physical forms are always changing, and that the nature spirits are working to bring all physical forms into a greater state of health, harmony, and beauty. (11) Be courageous in your beliefs and actions. (12) Learn to meditate if you don't already. In calm silence many answers come to you. (13) Pray as often as you can. The nature spirits receive the benefit of your prayers. (14) Have a good diet in order to keep up or restore a strong body and a sound mind.

You may actually pray more when you're not feeling good, but I'm sure you'd rather feel healthy. A good diet is important in keeping up good health. (15) Use violet-flame mantras and decrees such as "I am a being of violet fire; I am the purity God desires."

If you take all these actions, you are bound to help the angels and nature spirits to clean up the environment. A lot of the pollution in the world comes from the negative thoughts and actions of mankind that manifest as dirty rivers, lakes, oceans, and air, not to mention war and all sorts of interpersonal problems. Pollution is also a by-product of our industrial society, and technical solutions are needed, but the problem is much deeper than a mere mechanical problem. By helping the nature spirits, you will be helping to resolve the deeper problems.

RESOURCES

THE AUTOBIOGRAPHY OF A YOGI by Paramahansa Yogananda. Self-Realization Fellowship, 3880 San Rafael Ave., Los Angeles, CA 90065-3299 © 1974.
This classic book will enlighten you about the spiritual side of the world we live in as well as entertain you with the fascinating life story of a genuine yogi.

THE SCIENCE OF RELIGION by Paramahansa Yogananda.
Self-Realization Fellowship.
Yogananda gives a lucid account of how access to God is available to all of us .

THE SCIENCE OF THE SPOKEN WORD by Mark and Elizabeth Clare Prophet. Summit University Press, Box A, Livingston, MT 59047 © 1974.
This book explains the importance of and the how to of saying positive decrees. The Summit U. Press is the publishing arm of the Summit Lighthouse—source of much information about spiritual subjects, including nature spirits and the violet flame.

THE REAL WORLD OF FAIRIES by Dora Van Gelder. Theosophical Publishing House, 306 W. Geneva Rd., Wheaton, IL 60187 © 1977.
Dora gives a charming account of her clairvoyant observations of nature spirits.

FAIRIES AT WORK AND AT PLAY by Geoffrey Hodson. Theosophical Publishing House © 1982

Mr. Hodson gives his clairvoyant observations of nature spirits.

KINSHIP WITH ALL. LIFE by J. Allen Boone. Harper & Row, 49 East 33rd St., NY, NY © 1954.
Mr. Boone's classic story of how much he learned from "Strongheart" the German Shepherd "actor" dog, and how he extended that knowledge to feel his kinship with all life.

BEHAVING AS IF THE GOD IN ALL LIFE MATTERED by Machaelle Small Wright. Perelandra Ltd., Box 136
Jeffersonton, VA 22724 © 1983.
Machaelle Wright's life story and how she came to communicate with nature spirits. She has also published a workbook for cooperating with angel devas and nature spirits in the garden.

TALKING WITH NATURE by Michael J. Roads. H.J. Kramer, Inc., PO Box 1082, Tiburon, CA 94920 © 1985.
Mr. Roads tells how he came to hear the universal intelligence of God talking to him through rivers, trees, jade plants, various animals, and other forms of nature.

THE HEALING ENERGIES OF MUSIC by Hal A. Lingerman. The Theosophical Publishing House, Wheaton, IL 60187 © 1983 by Hal A. Lingerman.
Mr. Lingerman gives many examples of music that can be used for healing ourselves and our world.

THE SECRET POWER OF MUSIC by David Tame. Destiny Books, 377 Park Ave. South, NY, NY 10016 © 1984 by David Tame.
In this in-depth study, Mr. Tame analyzes the powerful effects music has on all of us.

YOUR BODY DOESN'T LIE by Dr. John Diamond. Warner Books Edition, published by arrangement with Harper & Row 10 East 53rd St. NY, NY 10022

This is one of the books that popularized behavioral kinesiology. It will give you a good introduction to kinesiology.

ADOPT A STREAM FOUNDATION, PO Box 5588, Everett, WA 98201
They will give you guidelines for adopting a stream or wetland. Send a self-addressed, stamped envelope and a small donation, if possible.

AMERICAN OCEANS CAMPAIGN, 725 Arizona Ave., Suite 102, Santa Monica, CA 90401.
They give information on protecting the ocean habitat.

AUDUBON, 950 Third Ave., NY, NY 10022.
Information on organizing youth groups for environmental education.

ECONET, 3228 Sacramento St., San Francisco, CA 94115.
International computer based communication system for environmental preservation.

GLOBAL RE-LEAF PROGRAM, American Forestry Association,
PO Box 2000, Washington, DC 20013.
For information on trees, contact them.

HUMAN ENVIRONMENT CENTER, 1001 Connecticut Ave. NW, Suite 827, Washington, DC 20036.
(202)331-8337. Clearinghouse and technical assistance center for youth conservation and service corps program.

KAP (KIDS AGAINST POLLUTION), Tenakill School, 275 High Street, Chester, NJ 07624.
(221)768-1332. This is a kids' networking group against pollution.
Send $6.00 to join network.

NATIONAL ARBOR DAY FOUNDATION, 100 Arbor Ave, Nebraska City, NE 68410. (402)474-5655.
Join this organization and receive free seedlings and information on trees.

NATIONAL COALITION AGAINST THE MISUSE OF PESTICIDES, 701 E Street SE, Suite 200,
Washington, DC 20003. (202)543-5450. They give information on alternatives to pesticides.

ISAAC WALTON LEAGUE, 1401 Wilson Blvd., Level B, Arlington, VA 22209.
Information regarding protection of natural resources.

AFTERWORD

I hope this little book will inspire you to take the reality of nature spirits seriously in a joyful way, and that you will keep them in your prayers and realize that they are always working for you, even if they remain aloof from direct contact with most humans.

A very important way for you to help them as well as yourself is to use the violet flame mantras for the transmutation of all errors of the past. The violet flame can be invoked from the heart of God. It comes from the violet ray out of the white light of Christ spirit. When you focus your loving attention on the violet ray, by saying a decree or mantra, it becomes a flame for transmutation. It is an efficacious way to clean up all sorts of poisons and pollutions in yourself and the planet. It is a spiritual fire that can work on the physical level - from the atomic and molecular on to macrocosmic levels.

The technique of how to use the violet flame is given by St. Germain through Mark and Elizabeth Clare Prophet, but is doesn't matter which religion or philosophy you follow; the violet flame is for everyone.

The nature spirits love to use the violet flame, and the more we invoke it on their behalf, the more they have available to clean up the environment.

If you would like to be on the mailing list for events, celebrations, seminars, and other publications concerning nature spirits, please send your name and address to the Golden Gnome Press, PO Box 189, Birch Tree, Mo 65438